Sharing Hearts and Loving Smiles

LINE ART PATTERN BOOK
by Annie Lang

If you're looking for love, you'll find plenty of hearts, happy kids and loving thoughts right here throughout the pages of this publication. You can share the love with dozens of mix and match designs from sweet little pixies, fun hearted kid characters, warmhearted bears, floral heart bouquets, pretty wordart messages and more.

Simply trace the design and then transfer the image onto your project surface to make outstanding personalized items with professional results every time.

Transferring the linework designs

Trace the design of your choice with pencil and tracing paper. Place transfer paper under the tracing paper and place onto your selected surface. Hold in place with tape if necessary. Retrace over the linework to transfer the design onto the project. For fabrics, trace the design, flip the pattern over and retrace the lines using a fabric transfer pen. Follow manufacturer's direction to iron the design onto your chosen fabric item.

Color or paint these designs with

Craft paints, watercolors, markers, coloring pencils, chalks, inks, fabric pens, paint pens, or crayons

These designs are great for

Home Dec Items like furniture, cabinets, accent items, walls, lamps, glassware, kitchen accessories, office and desk items, bathroom accents, cabinets, patio pots and outdoor items, etc.
Fabric and wearable items like t-shirts, sweatshirts, aprons, canvas shoes, totes, quilting squares, table linens and napkins, window and shower curtains, pillows, etc.
Paper Craft Projects like greeting cards, scrap page elements, tags, labels, stationery items, ornaments, gift bags, etc.

For more ideas and designer tips, please visit my Blog at

http://annielang-anniethingspossible.blogspot.com/
My Pinterest Board at http://www.pinterest.com/anniethings/
or my Facebook Page at
http://www.facebook.com/anniethingspossible

hearts
(C) Annie Lang anniethingspossible.com
hearts

(C) Annie Lang
anniethingspossible.com

(C) Annie Lang
anniethingspossible.com

LOVE
(C) Annie Lang
anniethingspossible.com

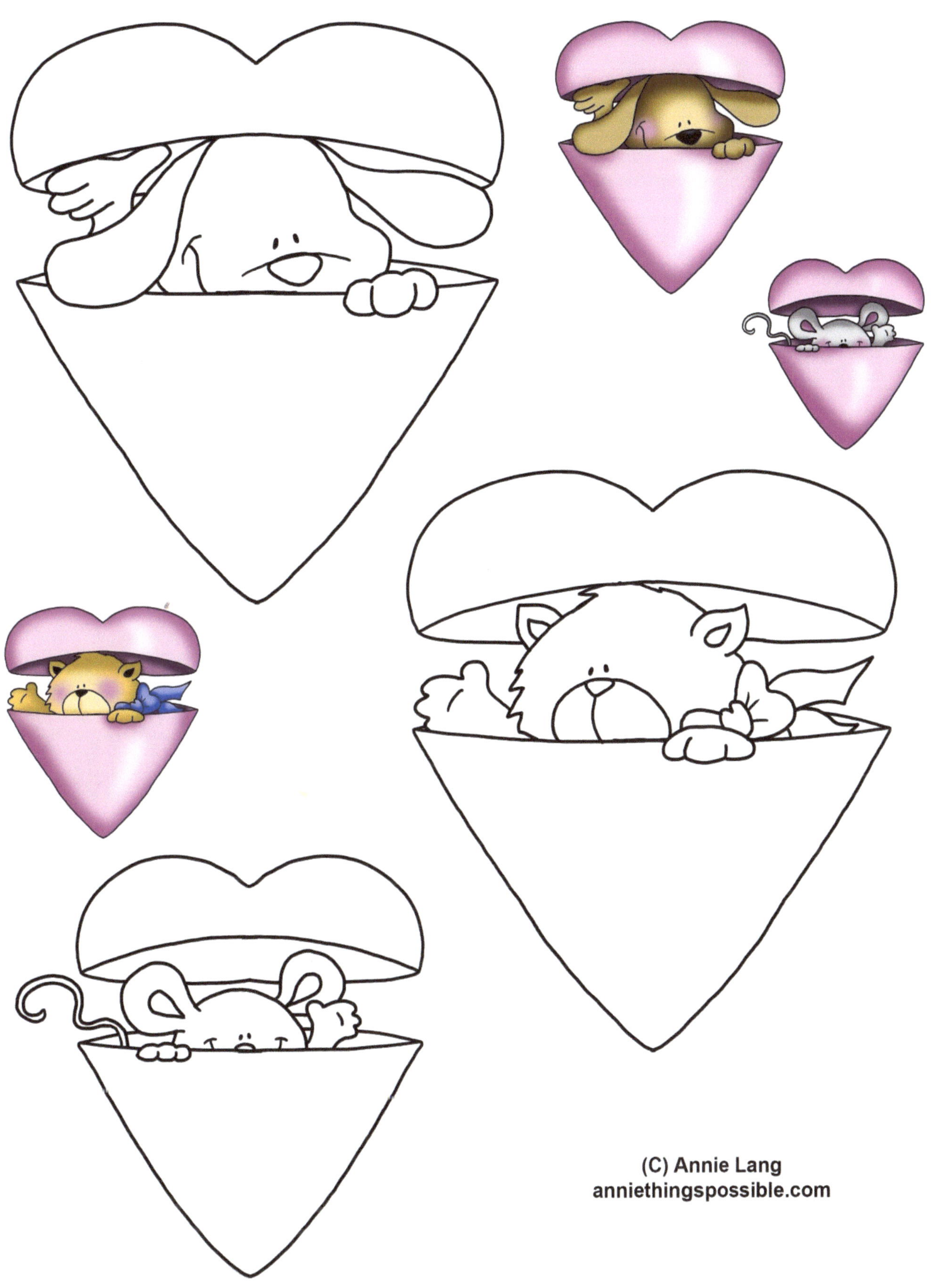

(C) Annie Lang
anniethingspossible.com

(C) Annie Lang
anniethingspossible.com

(C) Annie Lang
anniethingspossible.com

(C) Annie Lang
anniethingspossible.com

love multiplies

when you give it away

love multiplies

OXOXOXO

LOVE

LOVE

LOVE

LOVE

share your heart
share your smile
share your love

L
O
V
E

Love Cannot Be Measured

1 2 3 4 5 6 7 8 9 10

love sweet love

love one another

love live love

LOVE

(C) Annie Lang
anniethingspossible.com

(C) Annie Lang
anniethingspossible.com

(C) Annie Lang
anniethingspossible.com

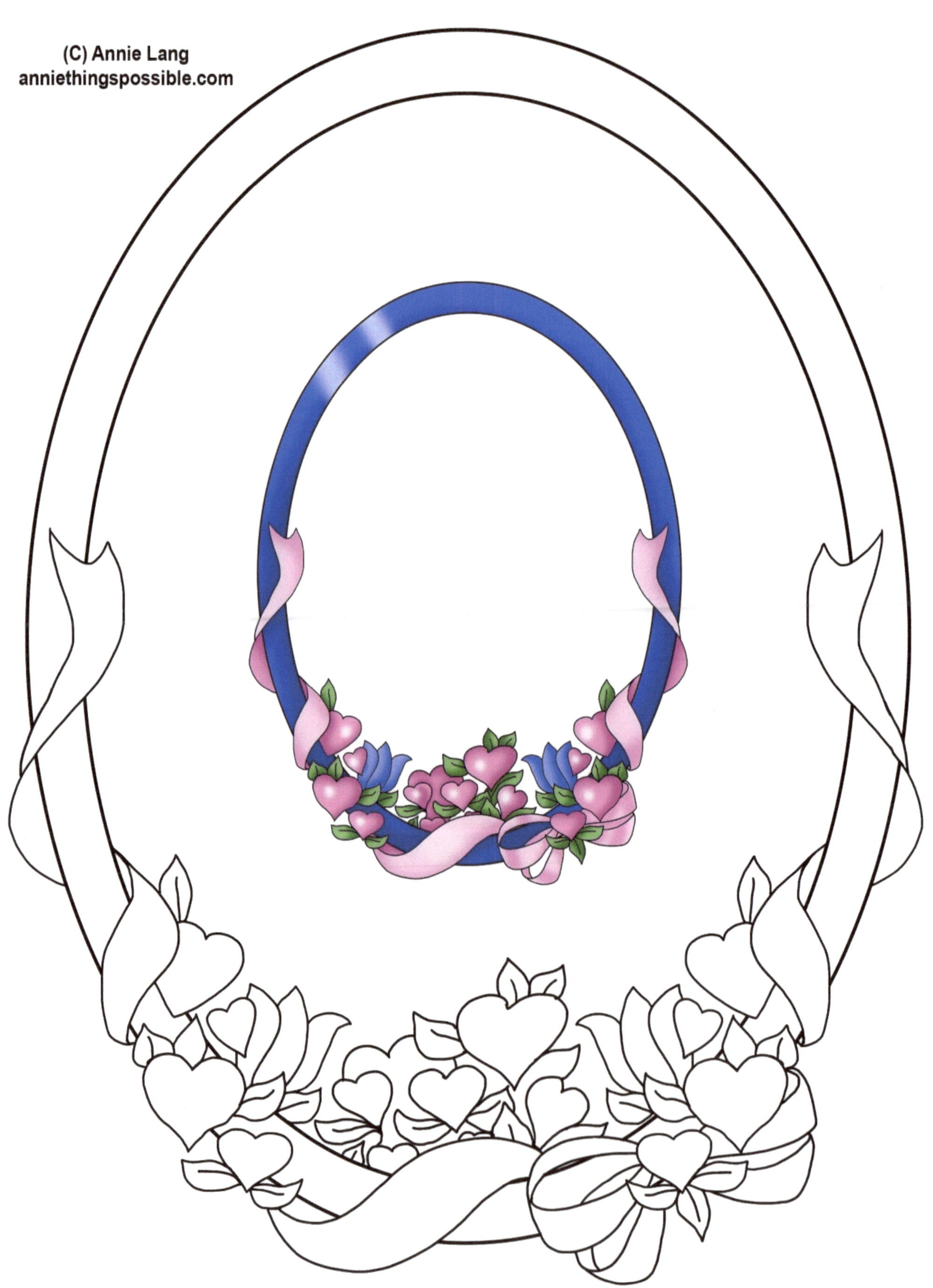

(C) Annie Lang
anniethingspossible.com

(C) Annie Lang
anniethingspossible.com

(C) Annie Lang
anniethingspossible.com

(C) Annie Lang
anniethingspossible.com

(C) Annie Lang
anniethingspossible.com

(C) Annie Lang
anniethingspossible.com
LOVE
LOVE

(C) Annie Lang
anniethingspossible.com

(C) Annie Lang
anniethingspossible.com

(C) Annie Lang
anniethingspossible.com

(C) Annie Lang
anniethingspossible.com

LOVE
LOVE
(C) Annie Lang
anniethingspossible.com

(C) Annie Lang
anniethingspossible.com

(C) Annie Lang
anniethingspossible.com
Put a
SMILE
in your
HEART
Put a
SMILE
in your
HEART

LOVE
is in the
AIR
LOVE
is in the
AIR
(C) Annie Lang
anniethingspossible.com

(C) Annie Lang
anniethingspossible.com

(C) Annie Lang
anniethingspossible.com

(C) Annie Lang
anniethingspossible.com

(C) Annie Lang
anniethingspossible.com

www.ingramcontent.com/pod-product-compliance
Lightning Source LLC
Chambersburg PA
CBHW040157240726
48664CB00002B/732